Easy Hymns for Ukulele

MW00680766

Book with Audio Access

By
Bert Casey

For Soprano, Concert, & Tenor Ukuleles
C Tuning (G, C, E, A)

Free Online Audio Access
Go to this address on the internet:

cvls.com/extras/ehu

Watch & Learn, Inc.

About This Book

This songbook features beginner to intermediate arrangements for classic hymns. The first arrangement you will learn for each song features a melody line along with the chord progression and the strumming pattern for ukulele. The second arrangement displays each song along with chord progressions, lyrics, and vocal melody lines. This is a great setup for sing-alongs because the lyrics are written in a large font so that multiple singers and musicians can read along.

Audio Tracks

This course also includes access to audio tracks to help you learn and practice. We have included three different recordings of each song. The first version features just the ukulele playing the strumming pattern along with the chord progression and a click track. The second version has the ukulele playing along with other instruments. The last recording features the other instruments with no ukulele so that you can practice playing the ukulele part in context.

You may access these files by going to the following web address:

cvls.com/extras/ehu/

The Author

Bert Casey, the author of this book, has been a professional performer and teacher in the Atlanta area for over 30 years. Bert plays several instruments (acoustic guitar, electric guitar, bass guitar, mandolin, banjo, ukulele, and flute) and has written seven instructional courses (*Acoustic Guitar Primer, Acoustic Guitar Book 2, Electric Guitar Primer, Bass Guitar Primer, Mandolin Primer, Flatpicking Guitar Songs, Ukulele Primer, Ukulele Chord Book,* and *Bluegrass Fakebook*).

Bert performed for several years in Atlanta and the Southeast with his bands Home Remedy and Blue Moon. His talent and willingness to share have helped thousands of students learn and experience the joy of playing a musical instrument.

More Ukulele Books

 If you need to brush up on your technique or expand your song repertoire, try the *Ukulele Primer* by Bert Casey. It starts off with the absolute basics like tuning (G, C, E, A), left and right hand position, and how to strum. You'll learn chords and different strum patterns in the context of fifteen popular songs. It includes 90 minutes of online Video instruction. Entertain your friends and family by learning how to play this great instrument that is soaring in popularity.

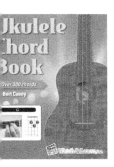 The *Ukulele Chord Book* contains over 300 chords with photos to illustrate how to play each chord. The accompanying diagram displays proper fret position, fingering, and labels the notes of the chord. Shows 12 common chord types in two different neck positions in all twelve major keys. Also includes sections on Moveable Chords, Common Chords in Each Major Key, and a full neck diagram of the ukulele with all notes labeled.

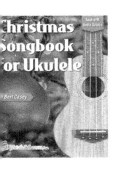 The *Christmas Songbook for Ukulele* with Online Audio Access features beginner to intermediate arrangements for classic Christmas songs. Each song features detailed strum patterns, chord charts, lyrics, and vocal melody notation. Section 2 displays each song with extended lyrics and chord progressions. This is a great for sing-alongs because the lyrics are written in a large font so that multiple singers and musicians can read along. This course also includes online access to audio tracks to help you learn and practice.

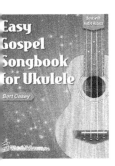 Learn how to play twelve more of your favorite hymns. The *Easy Gospel Songbook for Ukulele with Online Audio Access* is arranged just like the book you are currently reading. This companion songbook features: Amazing Grace, Blessed Assurance, Rock of Ages, Nearer My God to Thee, Shall We Gather at the River, Sweet By and By, The Old Rugged Cross, What a Friend We Have in Jesus, How Great Thou Art, In the Garden, Just a Closer Walk with Thee, Leaning On the Everlasting Arms.

All of these books are available at Amazon.com.

Table Of Contents

Section 3 - Lyrics

Appendix

Section 1
Getting Started

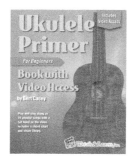

We are including the Getting Started Section from the *Ukulele Primer* course in case you need to brush up on your technique. If you find some of these songs and techniques too difficult, this is a great refresher course and is available on Amazon.com.

The Ukulele

There are four main types of ukuleles as shown by the photos below. This course will work with the Soprano, Concert, and Tenor ukes, all tuned G C E A.

The baritone ukulele is usually tuned like the first four strings of a guitar (D G B E) and will not be used in this course. I'll be using a tenor ukulele primarily, but you could use a soprano or concert uke with this course.

Soprano   Concert   Tenor   Baritone

Take your ukulele to your local music store to make sure it is in good playing condition and has good strings. If it needs any repairs, they can probably do it on the spot.

Get to know the folks at your local music store. They can be a great help with supplies, lessons, & advice.

Parts of the Ukulele

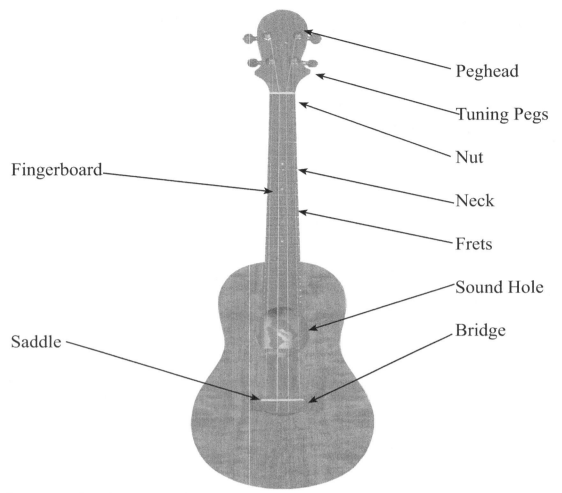

Peghead

Tuning Pegs

Nut

Fingerboard

Neck

Frets

Sound Hole

Bridge

Saddle

If you need to buy a ukulele, it is usually safer to purchase your first instrument from a reputable music store, who will make sure that the instrument is adjusted properly and offer service after the sale. Resist the temptation to buy a cheap plastic uke. These are little more than toys and can be very hard to play. You should purchase a case for your ukulele because many are broken by accident. There are several types of cases to pick from. You may buy a hard shell, which is most durable, a soft shell, or a gig bag. A case should keep the ukulele dry and protected when being transported.

Your ukulele should be stored in a neutral environment. This means not too cold, not too hot, not too wet, and not too dry. The wood in a ukulele is subject to change and will expand or contract in response to its environment. Too much of any of these conditions could cause permanent damage. For example, never leave your uke in your car for long periods of time during summer or winter months. Attics and basements tend to be poor locations for storing a ukulele as well.

Always use a case or gig bag when transporting your instrument from one place to another.

Tuning

There are several popular tunings for the ukulele. The two most common are the C tuning (G, C, E, A) and the A tuning (A, D, F#, B) with the C tuning being the most popular.

This course will use a soprano, concert, or tenor ukulele tuned to a C tuning (G, C, E, A). Tune the four strings of the ukulele to the same pitch as the four notes shown on the piano in the following diagrams.

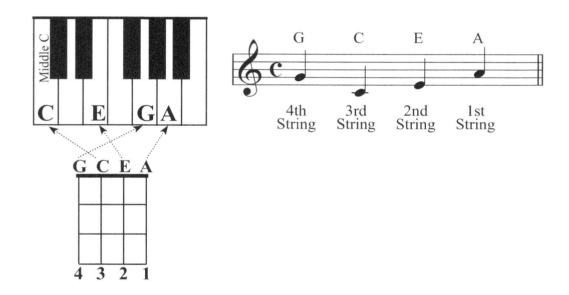

Electronic Tuner

An electronic tuner is the fastest and most accurate way to tune a ukulele. I highly recommend getting one. It may take months or years for a beginner to develop the skills to tune a uke correctly by ear. The electronic tuner is more precise and is used by virtually every professional player.

TIP *Never leave your instrument in a car or trunk during extreme heat or cold.*

Holding the Ukulele

Many ukulele players are self taught and have developed their own unique style and methods of playing. There is no one correct way to play the uke. I'll be showing you the most common techniques to use and the ones that I use.

At first you will be holding the ukulele sitting down. Use a straight back chair or stool so you can sit with good posture and have free arm movement without banging the uke on your arms or the furniture.

Sit erect with both feet on the floor. The ukulele should be braced against your chest with your right forearm so the neck doesn't move when you change hand positions. Press lightly with the right forearm to press the uke against your ribs. The left hand is used for balance.

The standing position is harder and takes a little more getting used to. Again, press the uke against your right side with your right forearm. You can use a ukulele strap if you like.

TIP *Always keep an extra set of strings in your case. You never know when you will break one.*

Left Hand Position

Arm Position

The left elbow should hang freely to the outside of the left leg. Make sure you aren't resting the left elbow on your leg. This will avoid undue stress on the elbow and wrist.

Thumb Position

You will see different players use different thumb positions, but I prefer this position because it allows you to play all of the chords without having to change your thumb position (Figure A).

The pad of your left thumb should be positioned on the center of the back of the ukulele neck. This will be our core position (Figure B).

Figure A   **Figure B**

Wrist Position

The wrist should be below the ukulele neck in a comfortable position. Don't strain your wrist to one side or the other (Figure C).

Fingernails

You will need to keep your fingernails trimmed so that you can easily press down on the fingerboard.

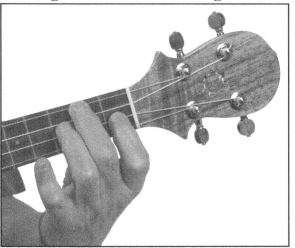

Figure C

Don't store your ukulele in the attic or basement. Extreme dryness or dampness can be bad.

11

Strumming

There are a variety of ways to strum the ukulele. You can use your thumb, your index finger, a felt pick, or fingerpick. I'll use the index finger for this course.

| **Thumb** | **Index Finger** | **Felt Pick** |

Index Finger Strum

Curl your right index (Figure 1). Place the thumb on the side of the first joint of the index finger (Figure 2). Strike the strings with the finger nail of your right index finger (Figure 3).

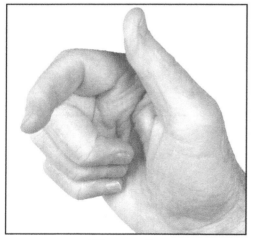 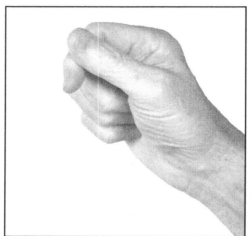 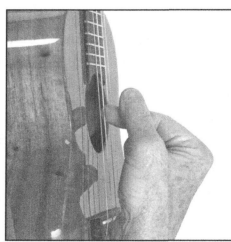

| **Figure 1** | **Figure 2** | **Figure 3** |

Right Hand Position

Position your right hand so that you strike the strings in the center of the sound hole. Don't brace your right hand on the ukulele. It should move freely with no part of the hand or wrist touching the ukulele. You should be moving from your wrist and not the elbow.

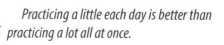
TIP
Practicing a little each day is better than practicing a lot all at once.

Ukulele Notation

The ukulele notation in this book is written on two lines or staves. The top staff is the melody line with lyrics. The bottom line is the strumming pattern for the right hand.

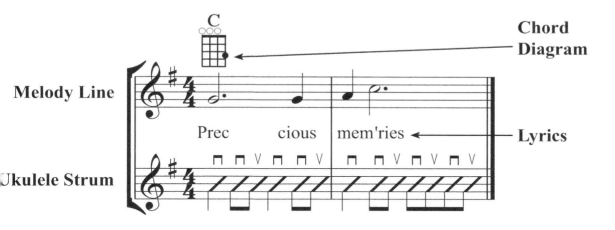

The exercises contain only one line or staff. This is the ukulele strumming notation.

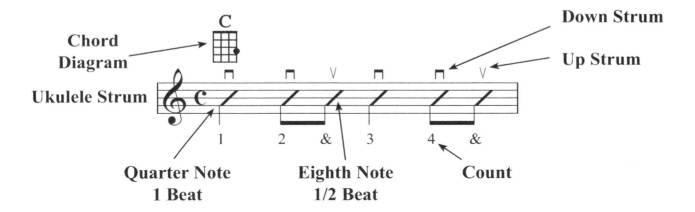

TIP

Practice new songs slowly and relaxed. Work on speed after you can play it perfectly.

Section 2
The Hymns

These songs are presented in order of easier to harder arrangements. Feel free to make the songs as simple or as complex as your playing level allows.

Online Audio Access is available at this address on the internet:

cvls.com/extras/ehu

Chord Diagrams

The first song is a five chord song in the key of G and we'll use the G, C, F, A, D, and Am chords. There are several ways to finger the D chord depending on your fingers size and dexterity.

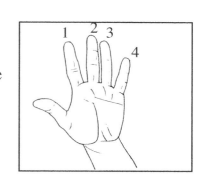

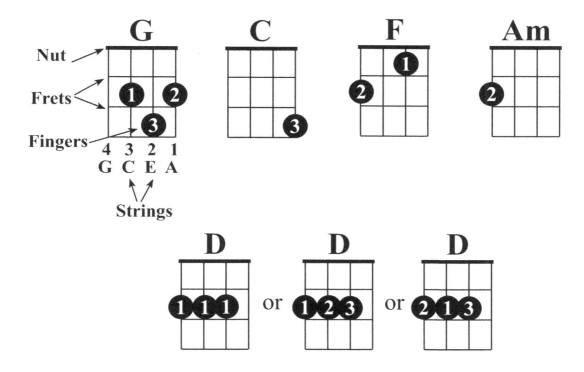

Strum Exercise

The first song is in 4/4 time, which means there are four beats per measure. This is a two measure strum and we count 1 2 & 3 4 & 1 2 & 3 & 4 &. The strum will be down down up down down up down down up down up down up.

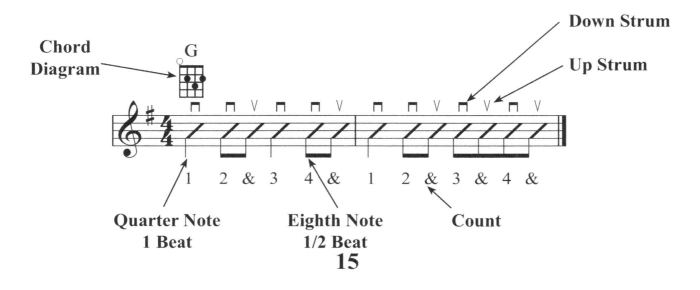

15

Precious Memories

Chords

Uncloudy Day is a three chord song in the key of G and we'll use the G, C, and D chords.

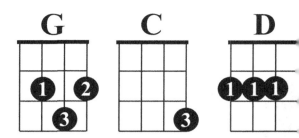

Strum Pattern

This song is in 4/4 time and we'll use 16th notes, which get 1/4 beat each. It will be counted 1 & 2 e & uh 3 & 4 e & uh. Pay close attention to the pick direction.

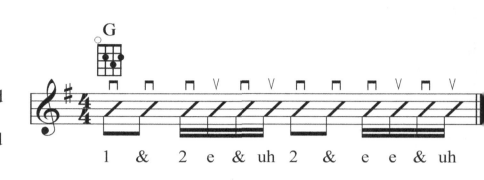

Uncloudy Day

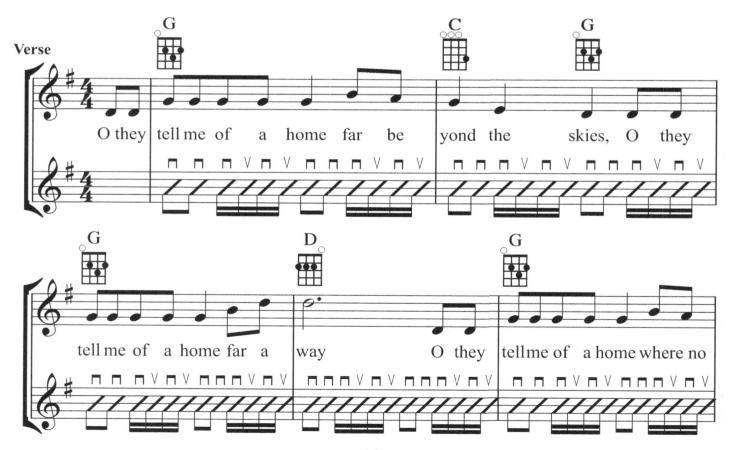

18

19

Chords

This is a four chord song using the G, C, D, and A chords

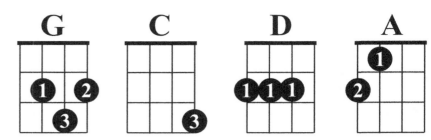

Strum Pattern

This song is in 4/4 time and uses two different strums throughout the song.

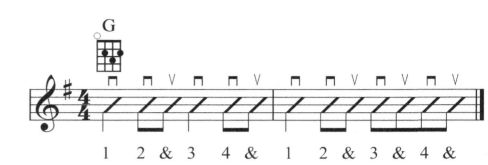

When the Roll is Called Up Yonder

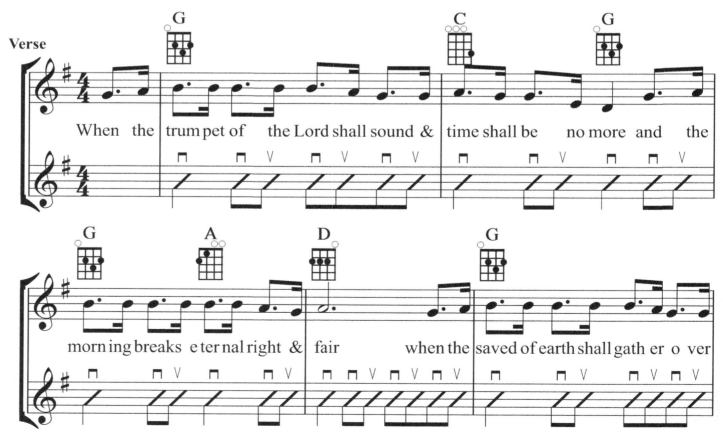

Verse

When the trum pet of the Lord shall sound & time shall be no more and the

morn ing breaks e ter nal right & fair when the saved of earth shall gath er o ver

21

Chords

Are You Washed in the Blood is in the key of G and we'll use the G, C, D, and A chords.

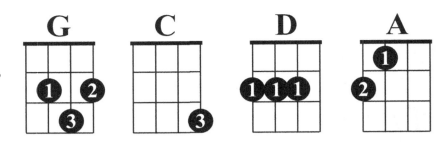

Strum Pattern

This song is in 4/4 time and uses the same strum throughout.

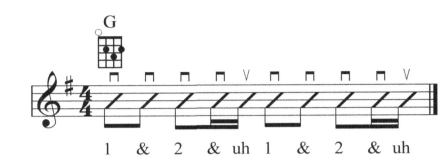

Are You Washed in the Blood

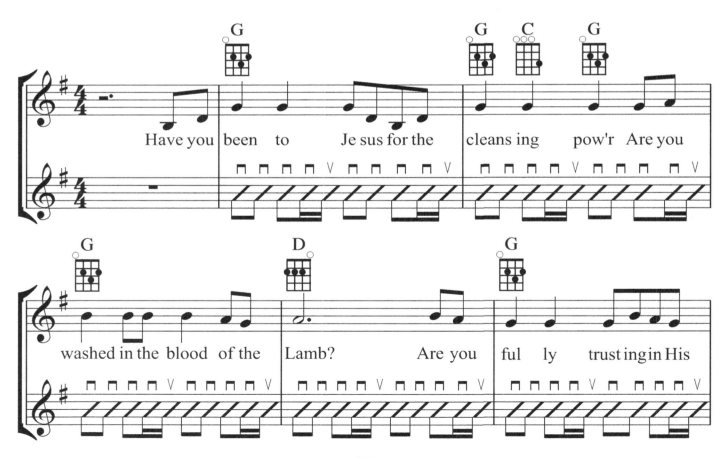

Chords

The next song is in the key of C and uses the C, G⁷, F, Dm, and F#dim chords

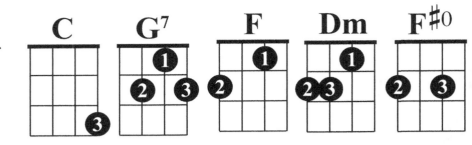

Strum Pattern

This song is also in 4/4 time and uses the same strum throughout except for bars 8 & 16 where you simply strum down three times..

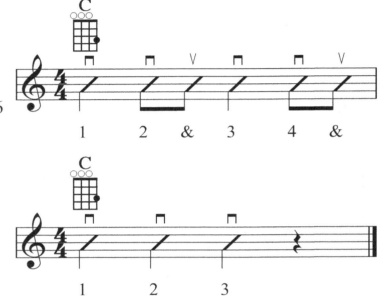

When We All Get to Heaven

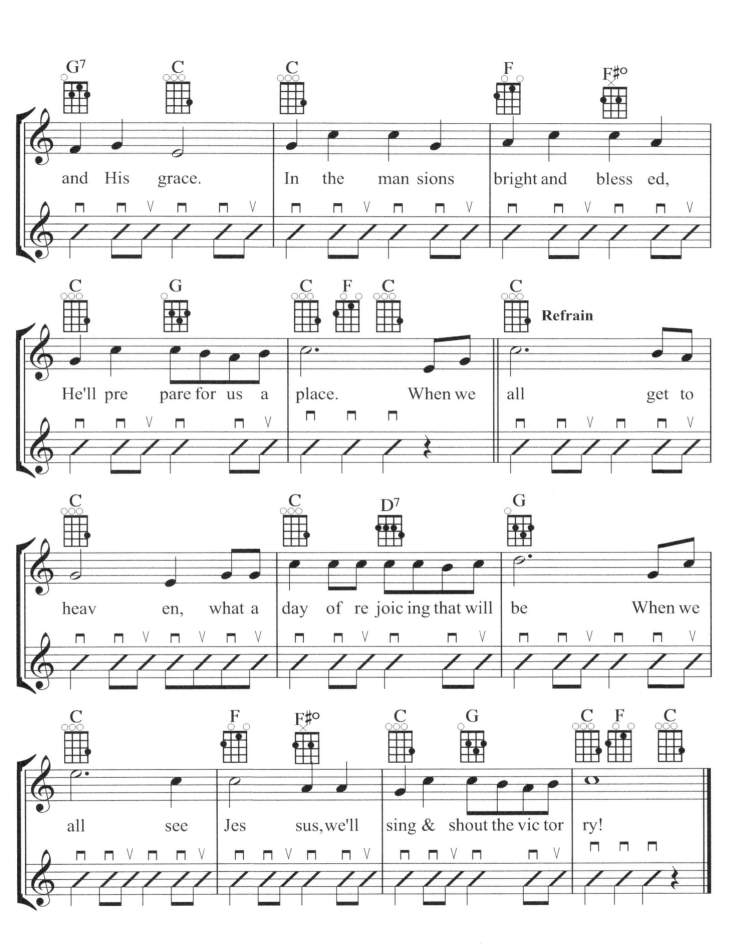

Chords

Here's another song in the key of C using the C, F, and G chords.

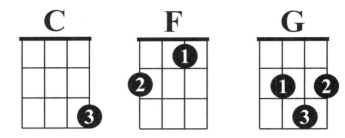

Strum Pattern

This is the first song in 3/4 or waltz time and has three beats per measure.

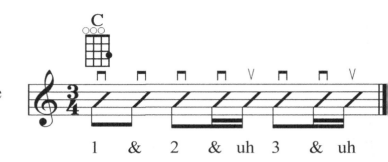

Come Thou Fount of Every Blessing

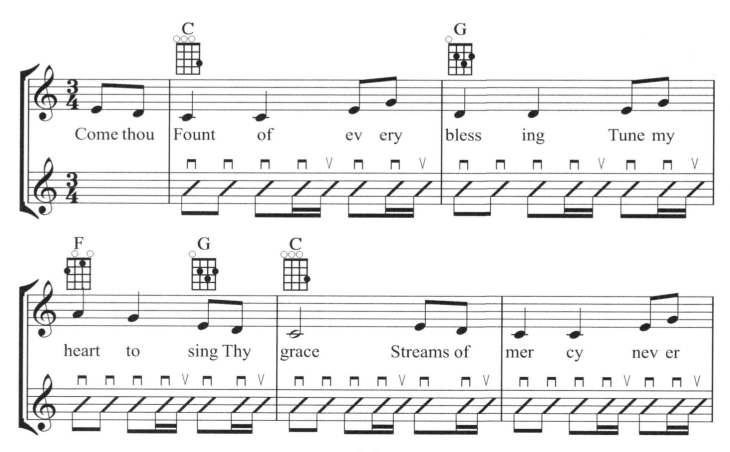

26

Chords

Back to the key of G and we'll use four chords, G, D, A, and D7.

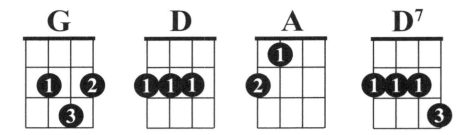

Strum Pattern

The next song is in 4/4 time and we'll use two different strums. You can vary these strums throughout the song.

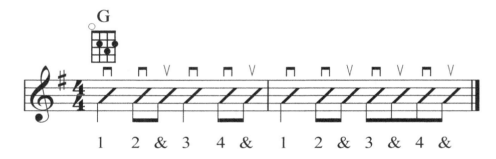

Glory Be to the Father

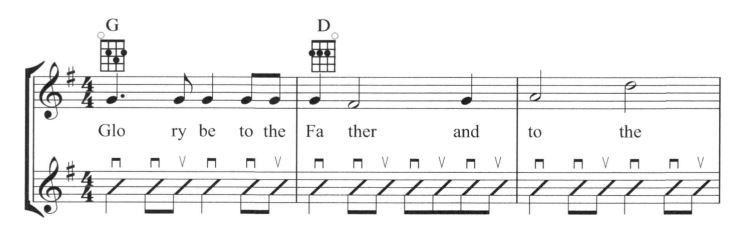

28

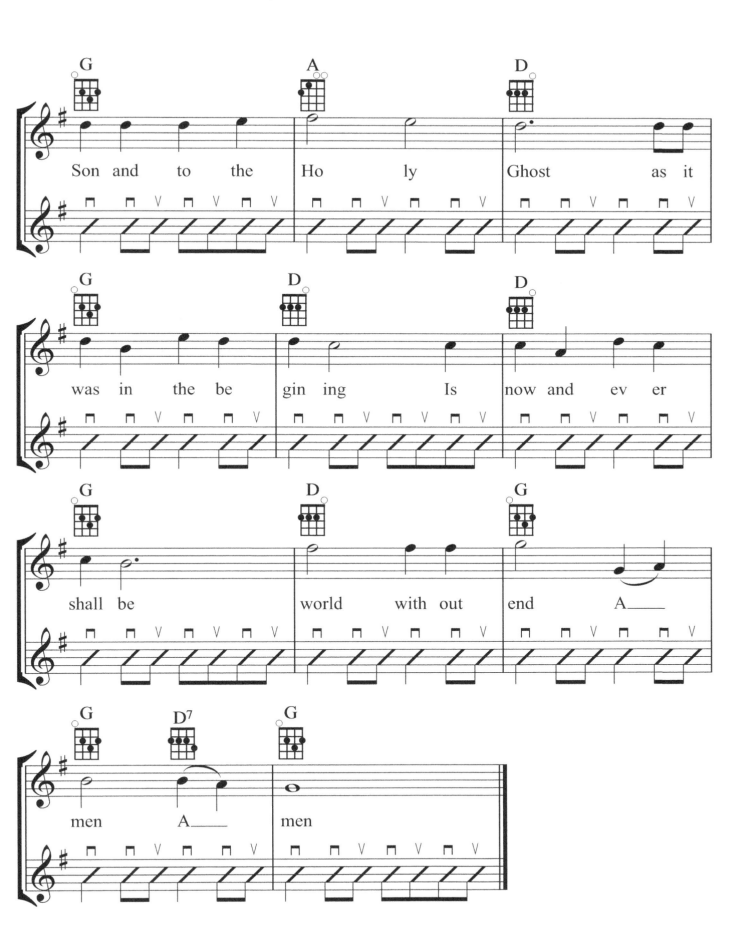

Chords

Four chords in the key of G using the G, C, D, and Em chords.

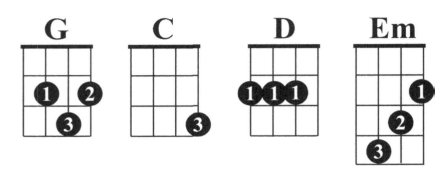

Strum Pattern

This song is in 4/4 time uses two strums.

1 & uh 2 & uh 3 & uh 4 & uh   1 & uh 2 & uh 3 & uh 4 e & uh

Do Lord

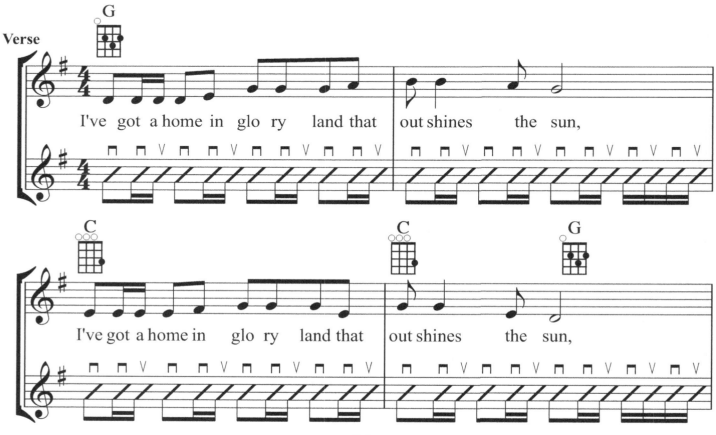

Verse

I've got a home in glo ry land that out shines the sun,

I've got a home in glo ry land that out shines the sun,

31

Chords

We'll use the same four chords in the key of G.

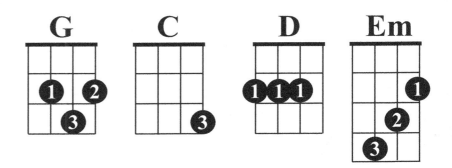

Strum Pattern

This song is also in 4/4 time and we'll use two different strums.

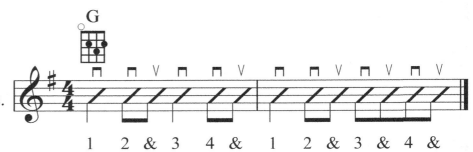

1   2   &   3   4   &   1   2   &   3   &   4   &

Swing Low Sweet Chariot

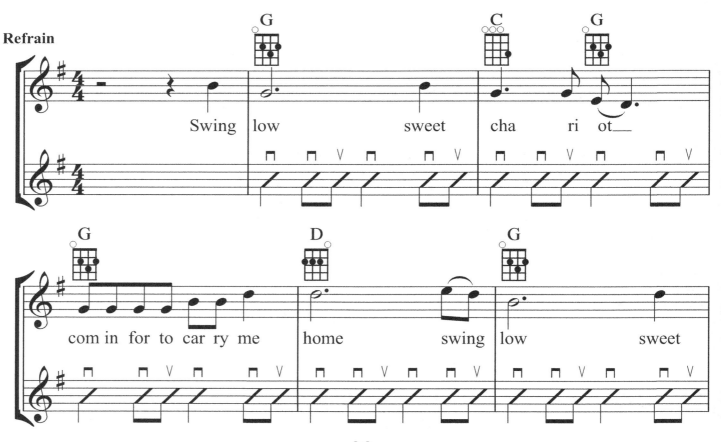

Refrain

Swing low   sweet   cha ri ot___

com in for to car ry me   home   swing low   sweet

33

Chords

Holy, Holy, Holy is in the key of C and will use the C, F, G, Am, and D chords.

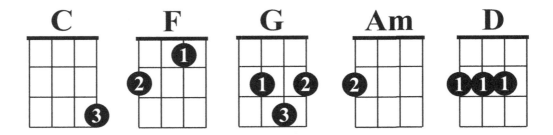

Strum Pattern

We've used these two strum patterns on several songs.

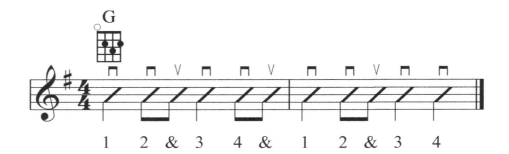

Holy, Holy, Holy

Chords

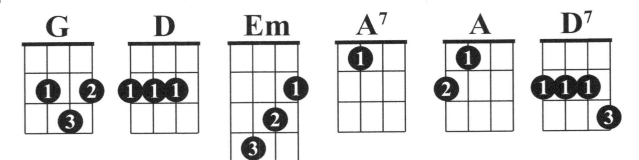

Strum Pattern

This song is in 4/4 time and uses a strum that we've used several times.

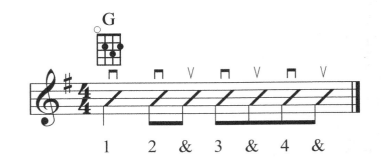

Go, Tell it on the Mountain

Verse

O When I was a seek er, I sought both night and day, I asked the Lord to

36

37

Chords

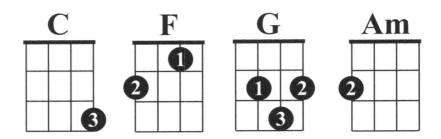

Strum Pattern

This song is in 4/4 time and uses two strums that are very similar.

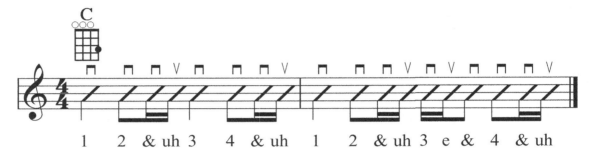

1   2 & uh 3   4 & uh   1   2 & uh 3 e & 4 & uh

Crown Him with Many Crowns

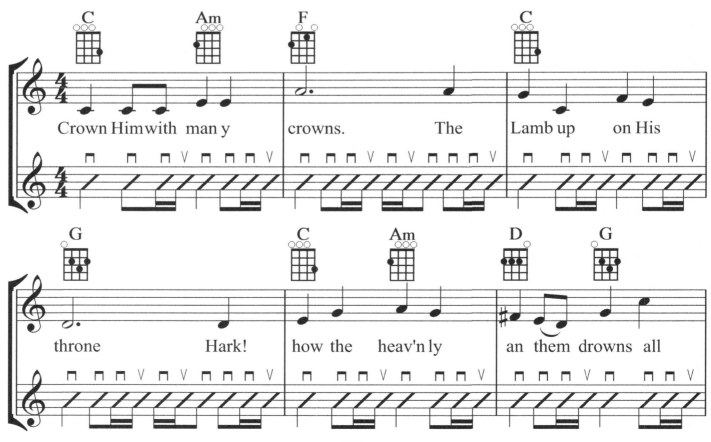

Crown Him with many crowns. The Lamb up on His throne Hark! how the heav'n ly an them drowns all

39

Section 3
Lyrics

This section contains the melody line, lyrics, and chord progressions so that you can play the complete version of the songs with all of the lyrics. This also works great for jam sessions or playing on stage because the lyrics are in a large font with the chord progression on each verse. This section is also arranged in alphabetical order to make finding the songs easier.

Are You Washed in the Blood

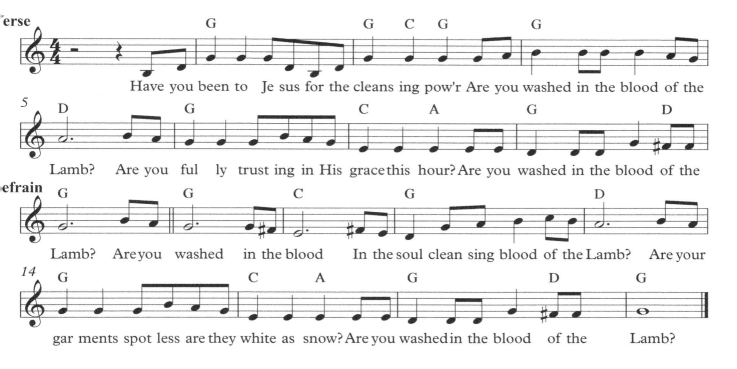

Have you been to Je sus for the cleans ing pow'r Are you washed in the blood of the Lamb? Are you ful ly trust ing in His grace this hour? Are you washed in the blood of the Lamb? Are you washed in the blood In the soul clean sing blood of the Lamb? Are your gar ments spot less are they white as snow? Are you washed in the blood of the Lamb?

Are you **G** walking daily by the Savior's **C** si**G**de
Are you **G** washed in the blood of the La**D**mb
Do you **G** rest each moment in the Cru**C**cifi**A**ed
Are you **G** washed in the bl**D**ood of the La**G**mb
Refrain

When the **G.** Bridegroom cometh will your **C** robes be **G** white
Are you **G** washed in the blood of the La**D**mb
Will your s**G**oul be ready for the **C.** mansions br**A.**ight
And be **G** washed in the bl**D**ood of the La**G**mb
Refrain

Lay as**G.**ide the garments that are **C** stained with **G.** sin
And be **G** washed in the blood of the La**D**mb
There's a f**G**ountain blowing for the **C** soul uncl**A**ean
O be **G** washed in the bl**D**ood of the La**G**mb
Refrain

Come Thou Fount of Every Blessing

Here I raise mine Ebenezer, hither by Thy help I'm come
And I hope, by Thy good pleasure, safely to arrive at home
Jesus sought me when a stranger, wand'ring from the fold of God
He to rescue me from danger, interposed His precious blood

Oh, that day when freed from sinning, I shall see Thy lovely face
Clothed then in the blood washed linen, how I'll sing Thy won-
drous grace
Come, my Lord, no longer tarry, take my ransomed soul away
Send Thine angels now to carry me to realms of endless day

O to grace how great a debtor daily I'm constrained to be
Let Thy goodness, like a fetter, bind my wand'ring heart to Thee
Prone to wander, Lord, I feel it, prone to leave the God I love
Here's my heart, O take and seal it, seal it for Thy courts above

Crown Him With Many Crowns

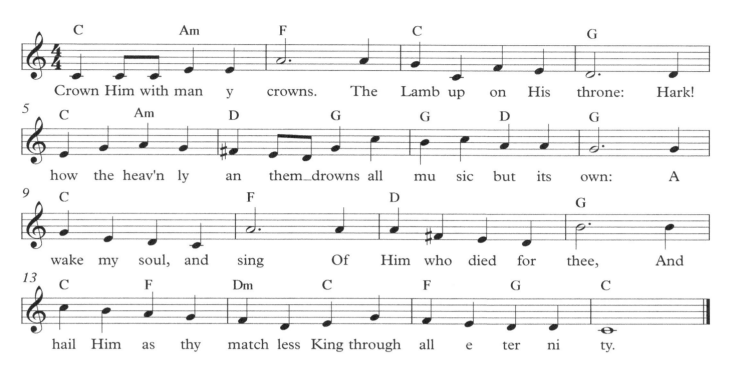

Crown Him with man y crowns. The Lamb up on His throne: Hark!

how the heav'n ly an them drowns all mu sic but its own: A

wake my soul, and sing Of Him who died for thee, And

hail Him as thy match less King through all e ter ni ty.

C   Am   F   C   C G
Crown Him the Son of God, Before the worlds began
And ye, who tread where He hath trod, crown Him the Son of Man
Who every grief hath known that wrings the human breast
And takes and bears them for His own, That all in Him may rest

Crown Him the Lord of life, Who triumphed o'er the grave,
Who rose victorious in the strife for those He came to save
His glories now we sing Who died, and rose on high
Who died, Eternal life to bring, And lives that death may die

Crown Him the Lord of heav'n, Enthroned in worlds above
Crown Him the king, to whom is given, the wondrous name of Love
Crown Him with many crowns, As thrones before Him fall,
Crown Him, ye kings with many crowns, He is King of all

Do Lord

G I took Jesus as my Savior you take Him too
C I took Jesus as my Savior you take Him **G** too
G I took Jesus as my Savior **G** you take Him **Em** too
G While He's **D** calling **G** you

Refrain

G Peter will be waiting with a welcome just for me
C Angels songs will fill the air through all eternit**G**y
G That will be a joyful everla**G**sting jubile**Em**e
Far a**G**way be**D**yond the bl**G**ue

Refrain

Glory Be to the Father

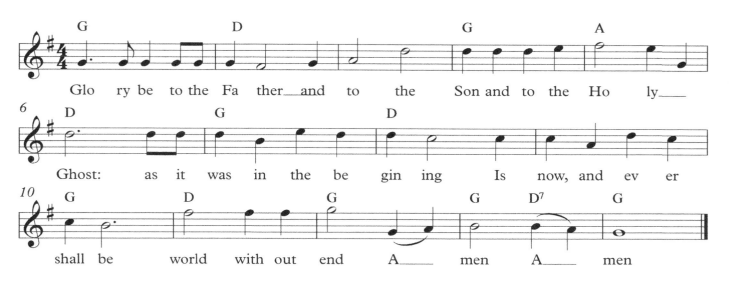

This hymn, also referred to as *The Doxology*, is commonly performed with no additional lyrics.

Go, Tell it on the Mountain

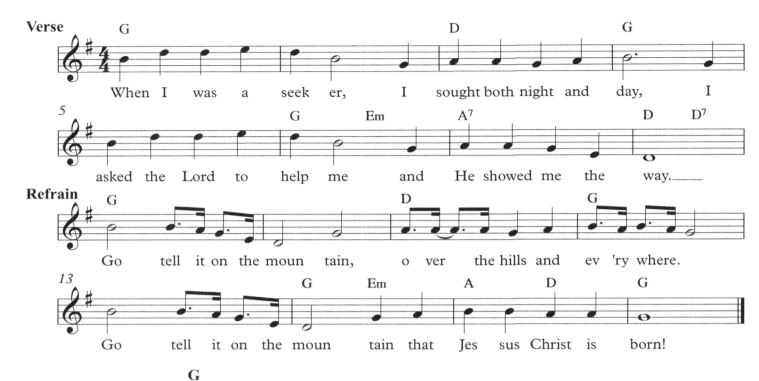

Verse

When I was a seek er, I sought both night and day, I
asked the Lord to help me and He showed me the way.

Refrain

Go tell it on the moun tain, o ver the hills and ev 'ry where.

Go tell it on the moun tain that Jes sus Christ is born!

While shepherds kept their watching
O'er silent flocks by night,
Behold throughout the heavens
There shown a holy light.
Refrain

The shepherds feared and trembled,
When lo! above the earth,
Rang out the angel chorus
That hailed the Savior's birth.
Refrain

Down in a lowly manger
The humble Christ was born,
And God sent us salvation
That blessed Christmas morn.
Refrain

Holy, Holy, Holy

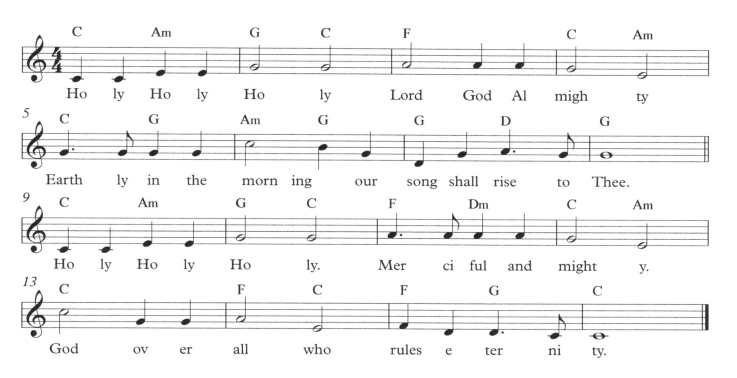

Holy Ho ly Ho ly Lord God Al migh ty

Earth ly in the morn ing our song shall rise to Thee.

Ho ly Ho ly Ho ly. Mer ci ful and might y.

God ov er all who rules e ter ni ty.

    C   Am   G C F   C   Am
Holy, Holy, Holy, All the saints adore Thee
    C   G   Am   G   D   G
Casting down their golden crowns around the glassy sea
    C   Am   G   C   F   Dm   C   Am
Cherubim and seraphim falling down before Thee
    C   F C   F   G   C
Who was and is and ever more shall be

    C   Am   G C F   C   Am
Holy, Holy, Holy, Through the darkness hide Thee
    C   G   Am   G   D   G
Through the eye of sinful man Thy glory may not see
    C   Am   G   C   F   Dm   C   Am
Only Thou art holy there is none beside Thee
    C   F C   F   G   C
Perfect in pow'r in love and purity

    C   Am   G C F   C   Am
Holy, Holy, Holy, Lord God Almighty
    C   G   Am   G   D   G
All thy works shall praise Thy name in earth and sky and sea
    C   Am   G   C F   Dm   C   Am
Holy, holy, holy, merciful and mighty
    C   F C   F   G C
God in three Persons, blessed Trinity

Precious Memories

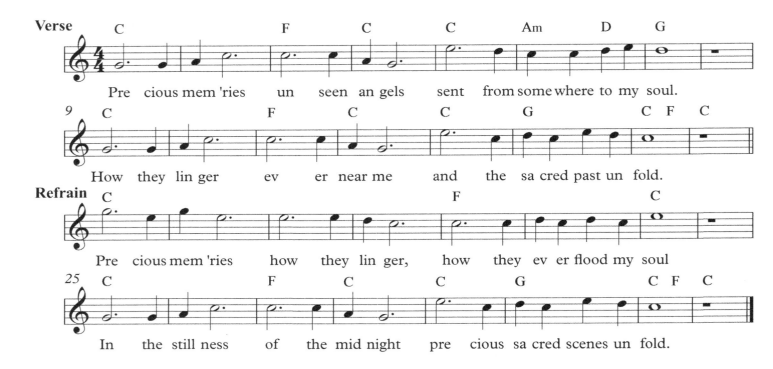

Verse

Pre cious mem 'ries un seen an gels sent from some where to my soul.

How they lin ger ev er near me and the sa cred past un fold.

Refrain

Pre cious mem 'ries how they lin ger, how they ev er flood my soul

In the still ness of the mid night pre cious sa cred scenes un fold.

C   F   C
Precious father, loving mother
C Am   D   G
Fly across the lonely years
C   F   C
To old home scenes of my childhood
C   G   C F C
In fond memory appears

Refrain

C   F   C
In the stillness of the midnight
C   Am   D   G
Echoes of the past I hear
C   F   C
Old-time singing gladness bringing
C   G   C   F C
From that lovely land somewhere

Refrain

C   F   C
As I travel on life's pathway
C   Am   D   G
I know what life shall hold
C   F   C
As I wander hopes grow fonder,
C   G   C   F C
Precious mem'ries flood my soul

Refrain

48

Swing Low Sweet Chariot

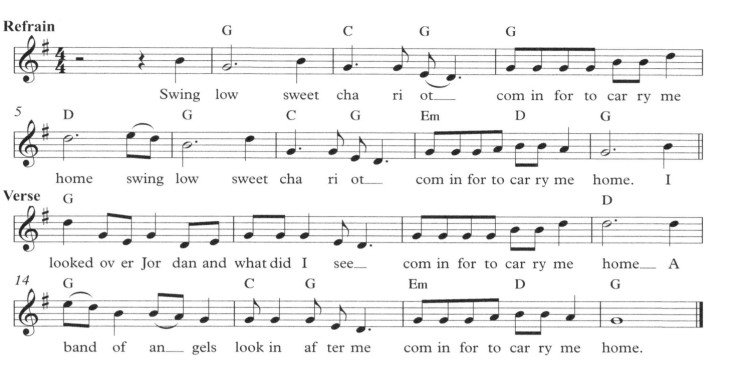

I looked over Jordan and what did I see
Coming for to carry me home
A band of angels coming after me
Coming for to carry me home
Refrain

If you get there before I do
Coming for to carry me home
Tell all my friends I'm coming, too
Coming for to carry me home
Refrain

I'm sometimes up and sometimes down
Coming for to carry me home
But still my soul feels heavenward bound
Coming for to carry me home
Refrain

Uncloudy Day

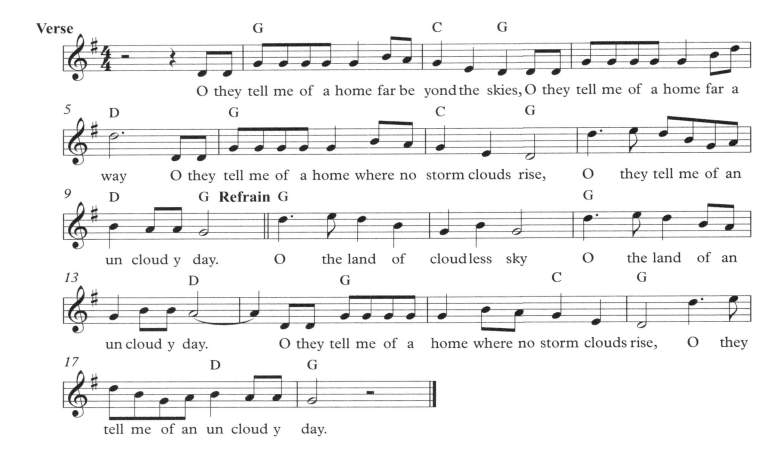

O they tell me of a home far beyond the skies, O they tell me of a home far away. O they tell me of a home where no storm clouds rise, O they tell me of an uncloudy day.

Refrain O the land of cloudless sky O the land of an uncloudy day. O they tell me of a home where no storm clouds rise, O they tell me of an uncloudy day.

O they tell me of a home where my friends have gone,
O they tell me of a land far away,
Where the tree of life in eternal bloom,
Sheds its fragrance through the uncloudy day
Refrain

O they tell me of a King in His beauty there,
And they tell me that mine eyes shall behold
Where He sits on the throne that is whiter than snow
In the city made of gold
Refrain

When the Roll is Called Up Yonder

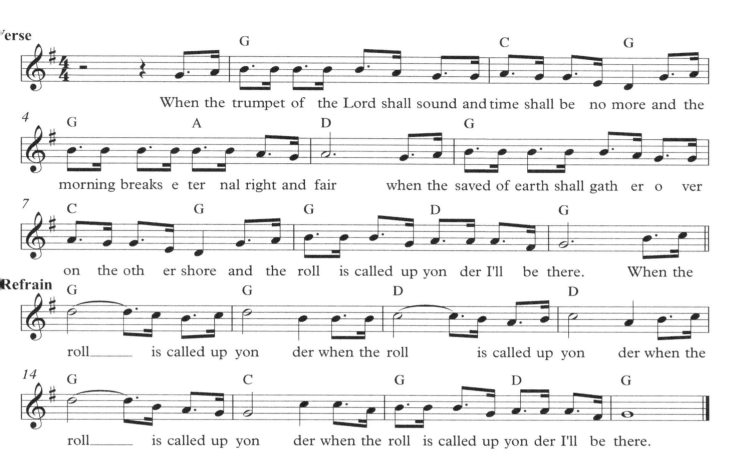

On that bright & cloudless morning when the dead in Christ shall rise
And the glory of His resurection share
When His chosen ones shall gather to their home beyond the skies
And the roll is called up yonder I'll be there
Refrain

Let us labor for the Master from the dawn till setting sun
Let us talk of all His wondrous love and care
Then when all of life is over and our work on earth is done
And the roll is called up yonder I'll be there
Refrain

When We All Get to Heaven

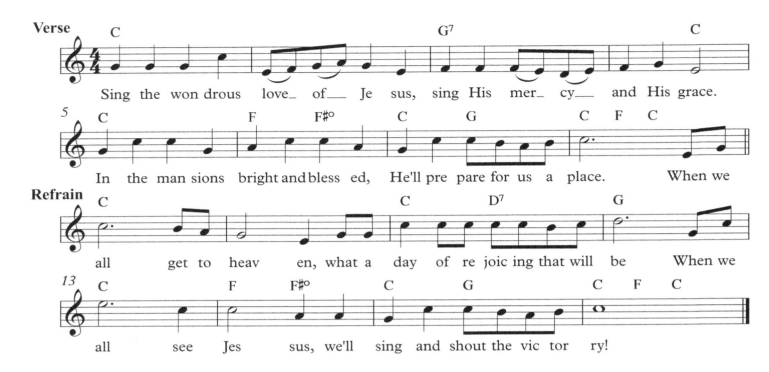

While we walk the pilgrim pathway clouds will overspread the sky
But when trav'ling days are over not a shadow not a sigh
Refrain

Let us then be true and faithful, trusting serving every day
Just one glimpse of Him in glory will the toils of life repay
Refrain

Onward to the prize before us. Soon His beauty we'll behold
Soon the pearly gates will open; We shall tread the streets of gold.
Refrain

Appendix

Chord Chart

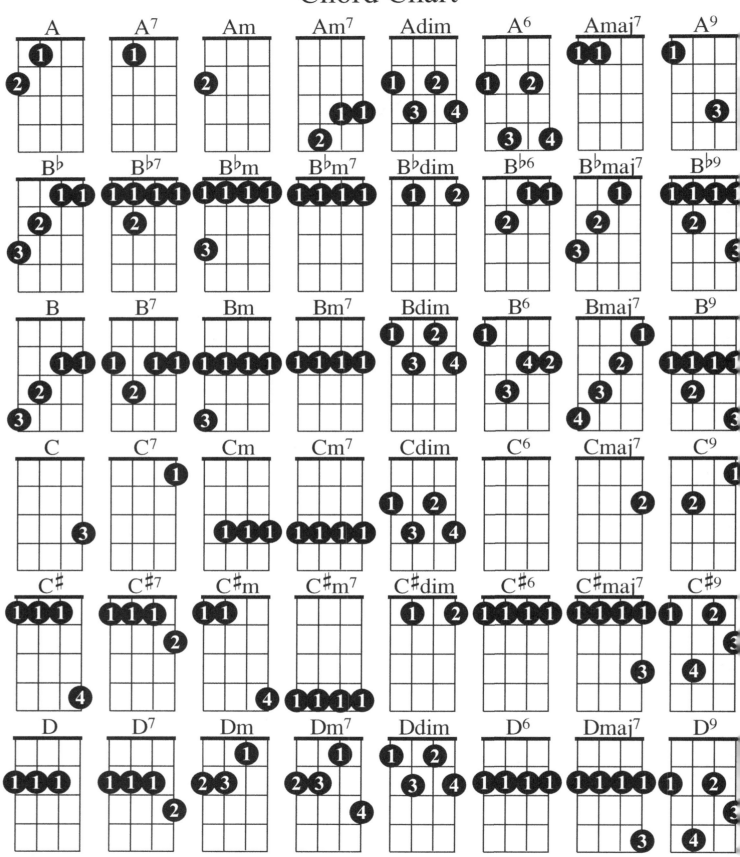

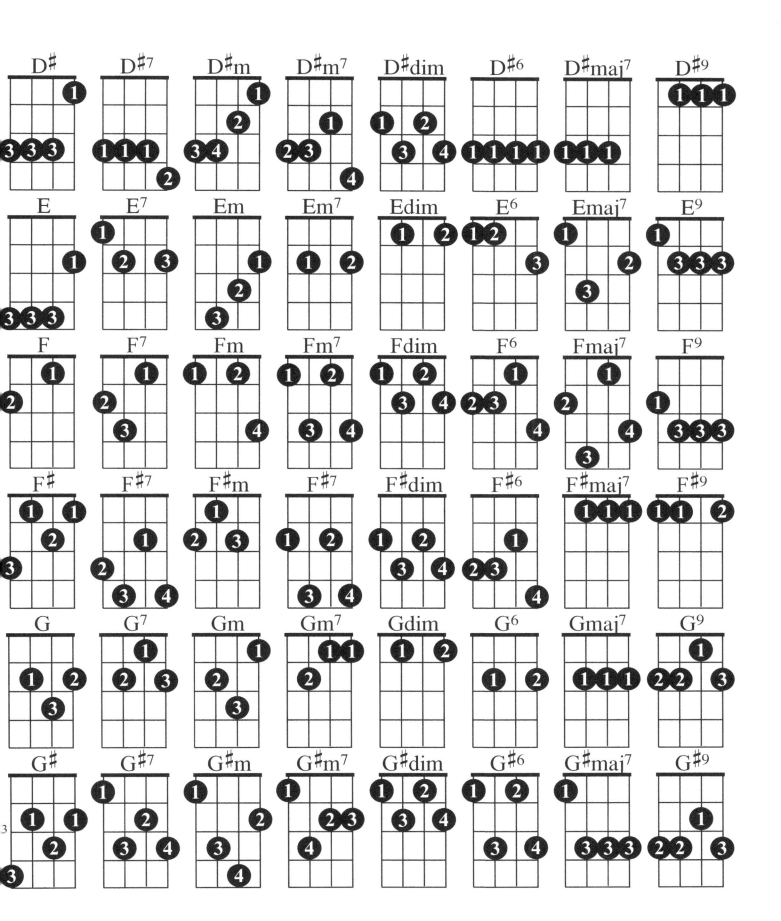

Made in the USA
Monee, IL
15 May 2021